YOUR GUIDE
TO NOT BE
~~STOOPID~~
~~STUPID~~

Published by: Kindle Direct Publishing
https://kdp.amazon.com/en_US/

All Scripture quotations, unless otherwise indicated, are taken from The New International Version (NIV)

(NIV) Holy Bible, New International Version®, NIV® Copyright ©1973, 1978, 1984, 2011 by Biblica, Inc.®

(NLT) Holy Bible, New Living Translation, copyright © 1996, 2004, 2015 by Tyndale House Foundation.

Copy Edited by Alyssa Myers
Cover design by Mike Badolato

International Standard Book Number: 9798395055521
Library of Congress Catalog Card Number: Pending

YOUR GUIDE TO NOT BE ~~STOOPID~~

~~STUPID~~

31 thoughts from the book
of Proverbs that will
make anyone wise

Mike Badolato

CONTENTS

CONTENTS

WHAT'S A PROVERB ANYWAY?

A proverb is a short saying that teaches a truth or a piece of advice. Proverbs are often based on common sense, experience or observation and are intended to provide practical guidance for living a wise, virtuous and successful life.

In the Bible, the book of Proverbs is a collection of wise sayings and teachings that provide practical guidance for living a godly life. The author of most of the book is King Solomon, who was known for his wisdom and understanding. The book is divided into 31 chapters, each containing a variety of proverbs on topics such as wisdom, morality, relationships, and work.

The book emphasizes the importance of seeking wisdom, living with integrity, and following God's commands. It also warns against the dangers of pride, laziness, and immorality. The book of Proverbs is a valuable resource for anyone seeking to live a godly life and make wise choices.

Throughout this 31-day devotional, you will be guided through a time of Scripture reading, observation, application, and prayer

DAY 1

"NOT SO SIMPLE"

Proverbs 1:4 NLT
These proverbs will give insight to the simple, knowledge and discernment to the young.

"NOT SO SIMPLE"

When I was a pre-teen, I used to go to my neighbor's house and play video games. (At this point in my childhood, I still didn't own a video game console... I know, shocking, isn't it?) Whenever my friend would do something his mom didn't like, she would say something that I never understood, "Don't be simple." Now in my undeveloped pre-teen brain, I always thought she was saying to her son, "Don't be easy." Obviously, that makes no sense, and it wasn't until years later that I realized that I was the "simple" one all along. You see, when his mom used the phrase, "Don't be simple," what she was really saying was, "Don't behave like you don't know better." This verse in Proverbs is telling us that if we take time to hear, learn, understand and practice the wisdom that is expressed in these proverbs, we won't be "simple." So take a few minutes right now to read through this chapter and identify areas in your life where you may be living like you don't know better.

PRAYER

Father in heaven, thank you for your Word which leads me into righteous living. Help me to identify and overcome the areas in my life where I am being, "simple." Amen.

DAY 2

"POWER OF TWO LETTERS"

Proverbs 2: 1-5

My son, if you accept my words and store up my commands within you, turning your ear to wisdom and applying your heart to understanding— indeed, if you call out for insight and cry aloud for understanding, and if you look for it as for silver and search for it as for hidden treasure, then you will understand the fear of the Lord and find the knowledge of God.

6

Have you ever thought to yourself, "If...?" If only I were a few inches taller... If I was from that family... If I had just started earlier....? We all have, and it is amazing to me how much power two little letters put together can have over a person. When I was a young man, I had what seemed like a promising soccer career that ended abruptly due to a knee injury. My biggest "if" was, "If I wouldn't have hurt my knee, where would my life be today?" Years after the injury, I was still wondering "what if." You see, there is great power in that two letter word. Proverbs 2 shows us that power. "If" you accept my words, "If" you call out for insight, "If" you look for it as silver, THEN! Whenever God gives us an "If," it comes with a "then." Here God is saying to us, "If you dedicate yourself to knowing my Word and my ways, then you will know me and my will for you." What a powerful proposition that starts with two little letters, "if." So, "if" you will commit yourself to the pursuit of the wisdom and ways of God, "then," you will know Him.

PRAYER

Father in heaven, I thank you for the opportunity to know you in a deep and intimate way. I understand the power of "if" statements and I am ready to see Your "then." Help me to commit my life and heart to knowing Your ways, understanding that as I do, I will know you. Amen!

DAY 3

"A STRAIGHT SHOT"

Proverbs 3: 5-6
Trust in the Lord with all your heart and lean not on your own understanding; in all your ways acknowledge Him, and he will make your paths straight.

"A STRAIGHT SHOT"

When I first gave my life to Jesus, I was in a discipleship program called Teen Challenge. One of the many ways we were discipled was by completing different workbooks called, Personal Studies for New Christians (PSNCs).

One of the more challenging requirements for me in completing these PSNCs was Scripture memorization; with each book, you had to memorize some Bible verses and be able to write them out. The first bible verse I ever memorized after giving my life to Jesus was this one, Proverbs 3: 5-6. This verse has encouraged, challenged and directed me more times than I can count over the past 9 years, but I want to share with you just one of those occasions.

During my time of ministry training, I began to become very impatient. I felt as though I was ready to move into a new season of life in which I would be in a pastoral role at a local church. I remember very clearly being in prayer at the Teen Challenge house, complaining to God about how I was sick of waiting and was ready to do what I knew He was calling me to do. This verse came to mind, and the reality and understanding that God makes our path straight might as well of smacked me in the face.

You see, the shortest distance from one place to another is a straight line. If this verse is telling me that if I trust the Lord with all my heart, don't take matters into my own hands, and set Him as the priority, then He will make my path straight. In other words, God has placed me on a straight path, with no detours, ready to arrive on time - the shortest distance from where I am to where I am going!

PRAYER

Father in heaven, thank you that you know all things and do all things well and on time. I ask you to help me today to trust you in a measure I have never trusted before, knowing that as I do, you are guiding and directing me.
Amen!

DAY 4

"WHAT DOES THAT EVEN MEAN?"

Proverbs 4:23

Above all else, guard your heart, for it is the wellspring of life.

We, as Christians, have a lot of sayings that make no sense without context. "Guard my heart? What does that even mean?" Well, let me break it down for you.

Our heart is the center of who we are. It's where our emotions, thoughts, and desires come from. If we're not careful, our hearts can be easily influenced by the world around us. That's why it's so important to guard it. Think of your heart like a garden. If you don't tend to it and protect it, it will become overrun. On the flip side, if you take care of it, it will flourish and produce beautiful fruits and vegetables.

So, how do we guard our hearts? Well, the starting point for everything in the Christian life is God's Word. We must fill our hearts with the Word of God. The more we saturate ourselves in Scripture, the less room there is for ungodly and worldly influences to take root. We also need to be mindful of the company we keep. Surrounding ourselves with godly people who will encourage and challenge us in our faith is crucial.

Lastly (and mind you, this is not an exhaustive list), we need to be intentional about what we allow into our hearts. This means being careful about the many forms of media and entertainment we consume, the conversations we have with others and the thoughts we entertain. So, let's make it our mission today and every day to guard our hearts. When we do, everything we do will flow from a place of love, joy, and peace and who doesn't want more of that in their life?

PRAYER

Father in heaven, thank you for being the Giver of new hearts. I ask you to help me to be diligent in keeping my heart guarded from any bad influence. Help me to keep my heart pure towards you and others. Amen!

DAY 5

"AN OPEN BOOK"

Proverbs 5:21
For a man's ways are in full view of the Lord, and he examines all his paths.

"AN OPEN BOOK"

Years ago, I heard someone say that we are all three people: the person we are in public, the person we are in private, and the person we are in secret. In public settings, it is easy for us to present a version of ourselves that may or may not be completely honest. In private, this is a little more difficult; our private selves are the ones that only close family and friends know and see. Nothing like a spouse or siblings to tell us who we really are. Am I right, or am I right? But then there is this final self, the secret self. This is the one that conceals our deepest pains and shortcomings, even from those who are closest to us. This is the self that keeps our fears and worries away from the public and private world. As desperately as we may try to keep the world around us from knowing our private life, nothing is hidden from God. This proverb clearly shows us that our lives are like an open book for God. Now, this can be a comforting truth, or it can be a truth received with great fear and anxiety. I mean, who wants their deepest darkest secrets exposed? No one! When we know the character and nature of God, we receive this as a great comfort knowing that God sees our faults and fears and speaks "grace" to them. Grace to forgive your secrets and grace to empower you to overcome your fears. Today, allow God to examine you, your fears, your secrets, and your pains, and receive His grace!

PRAYER

Father in heaven, I understand that nothing is hidden from you every fear and area of sin in my life is exposed before you. Help me to allow your Spirit to examine me and empower me. I ask for your forgiving grace for areas of sin in my life and I receive it by faith. Amen!

DAY 6

"UP AND AT 'EM"

Proverbs 6: 9
"How long will you lie there, you sluggard? When will you get up from your sleep?"

Now, if you are anything like me, you love your "beauty sleep," but this verse is a reminder that there's a time and a place for everything and sometimes, that means it's time to get "up and at 'em."

We all have responsibilities and tasks that need to be accomplished, whether it's going to work, taking care of our families or serving at our churches or in our communities. I know it's tempting to hit snooze and stay in bed (I am the guy who sets an alarm for every five minutes for thirty minutes leading up to my actual wake-up time, just so I can feel like I slept in, even though I didn't), but we need to remember that our actions have consequences; if we don't put in the work now, we won't reap the rewards later.

There is always good news in the Kingdom of God, so here is some good news: when we put in the work, we can experience the satisfaction of a job well done and enjoy the fruits of our labors.

So, let's not be sluggards as the Bible puts it. Let's get "up and at 'em" and handle our business.

PRAYER

Father in heaven, I come before you seeking your guidance and strength. Help me overcome laziness and embrace diligence so that I can be successful and fulfill the purpose you have for my life. Amen!

DAY 7

"LED BY LISTENING"

Proverbs 7: 21
With persuasive words she led him astray; she seduced him with her smooth talk.

"LED BY LISTENING"

When reading this proverb, I can't help but think about the story of Adam and Eve in Genesis. Remember the story? God gave Adam a command not to eat the fruit of the tree of the knowledge of good and evil. Then God created Eve so Adam would not be alone. Eve then engages in a conversation with the serpent and is led astray, she eats from the tree from which they were commanded not to eat, and sin enters the world.

This proverb and the story in Genesis shows the danger of listening and being influenced by the words of the wicked. Today, I can't imagine a serpent coming and talking to you, but an ungodly man/woman, that's a different story. We must be careful not to allow the voices of the world, culture, news, social media, etcetera, to influence us. We are called to influence the world for Jesus, not be influenced by the world.

We tend to be led by what we listen to, so let's listen to the truth.

PRAYER

Father in heaven, if I am allowing the "voices" of the world to influence me, please show me and forgive me. Give me wisdom in how to remove these influences and help me to hear your voice today. Amen!

DAY 8

"FIND 'ME'"

Proverbs 8: 35
"For those who find me find life and receive favor from the Lord."

When you read this verse, you might have been wondering, "Who is 'me'?" Well, strangely enough, in this verse, "me" refers to wisdom. Let me tell you something I have found out the hard way on too many occasions; wisdom is a pretty big deal.

Wisdom is more than just knowledge or intelligence. It's the ability to discern what is right and not just to be able to discern it but to actually do it!

Think about it like this: when we make wise choices, we're more likely to experience success, joy and peace in our lives and when we're living in alignment with God's will, we can trust that He will bless us and guide us along the way. Wisdom, like everything worth anything, doesn't just fall into our laps; we have to actively seek it out.

So, let's be people who read God's Word, seek counsel from mentors, and pray for discernment, because when we do, we will "find 'me'" or we will find wisdom and receive favor from the Lord. And who couldn't stand to have a little more of that in their life?

PRAYER

Father in heaven, I surrender my life to you, seeking to walk in the wisdom and understanding that comes from honoring and obeying your Word. Amen!

DAY 9

"RECEPTION OF CORRECTION"

Proverbs 9: 8
Do not rebuke a mocker or he will hate you, rebuke a wise man and he will love you.

"RECEPTION OF CORRECTION"

I can tell if you really love me by how you respond to my cliffhanger. I am not talking about your favorite show on Netflix ending an episode at a high point, leaving you in suspense and needing to know what is going to happen next. The cliffhanger I am talking about is much more gross than that. I am talking about a boogie that is dangling out of someone's nose (don't act like it has never happened to you, you're not too good to get a cliffhanger). You see, if you let me walk around knowing that thing is dangling out of my face, I know you don't love me, but if you are willing to deliver some uncomfortable news to me about the state of my nostrils, I know you truly care for me and I will in turn love you for that.

You were willing to be uncomfortable for my benefit. This verse in Proverbs shows us that wise people will receive correction and love the corrector for it. When we know that someone is willing to be uncomfortable to make us better, we can receive correction from a wise person.

PRAYER

Father in heaven, as difficult as correction can be help me to give and receive it as a wise person and from a place of love. Amen!

DAY 10
"MY WAY"

Proverbs 10: 8
"The wise in heart accept commands, but a chattering fool comes to ruin."

No one's favorite thing in life is being told what to do. We all want to be in control of our own lives and make our own decisions, but this verse reminds us that there's wisdom in accepting commands.

Think about it this way: when we're open to receiving guidance and instruction, we're more likely to make good choices and avoid making mistakes. When we're willing to learn from others, we can grow in wisdom and maturity.

On the other hand, when we're stubborn and refuse to listen to anyone else, we're setting ourselves up for failure.

So, let's be wise and open to accepting commands. Let's seek out wise counsel from trusted mentors and be willing to learn from our mistakes. Because when we do, we can avoid the pitfalls of foolishness and walk in the path of wisdom.

PRAYER

Father in heaven, I pray for a wise and discerning heart that embraces your commandments and walks in integrity, that my words may be a source of blessing and encouragement to others. May my actions bring honor to your name and be a testament to your goodness. Amen!

DAY 11

"NOT YOUR FRUIT"

Proverbs 11: 30
The fruit of the righteous is a tree of life, and the one who is wise saves lives.

"NOT YOUR FRUIT"

Now, I know what you're thinking, "not your fruit." "What does that even mean?" One of the most powerful moments in my life happened when I realized my fruit isn't for me; it is for those around me. Of course, I am talking about spiritual fruit.

When we live a righteous life, we bear fruit that brings life to others. This fruit can take many forms, such as acts of kindness, words of encouragement, or simply being a good listener. And when we share this fruit with others, we can bring hope and joy into their lives.

But here's the thing: we can't do it alone. We need wisdom to know how to best use our gifts and talents to serve others and when we use our fruit to help others we can save lives in more ways than one.

Think about it this way: when we offer a listening ear to someone who is struggling, we can help them feel heard and understood. When we offer a helping hand to someone in need, we can make a tangible difference in their life. And when we share the love of Jesus with others, we can offer them eternal life.

PRAYER

Father in heaven, I pray for a heart that seeks to refresh and nourish others. Use me as an instrument of your love and light, that I may bear fruit that lasts for eternity. Amen!

DAY 12

"WIN WITH WORDS"

Proverbs 12:14
*From the fruit of their lips people are
filled with good things, and the work
of their hands brings them reward.*

Who doesn't want to be successful in life? We all want to achieve our goals, make a difference in the world, and be recognized for our hard work, but this verse reminds us that success comes from more than just our actions - it also comes from our words. So, it could be said, "We win with our words."

When we speak words of kindness, encouragement, and wisdom, we can fill others with good things. We can lift them up, inspire them, and help them see the best in themselves. And when we do, we not only bring other joy, but we also reap the rewards of our own positive words.

Now the danger with this is words can be easy and we can just be giving lip-service. Our words have to be backed up by action. We can't just talk the talk - we have to walk the walk. When we work hard, use our talents, and make a difference in the world, we can reap the rewards of our labor.

So, let's be intentional about both the words we speak and the actions we take. Let's use our words to bring good things into the world and our hands to do the work that brings us reward. Because when we do, we win with our words.

PRAYER

Father in heaven, I humbly pray that my words may be filled with wisdom, kindness, and grace, bringing blessings and edification to others. May my speech reflect your truth and love, and may it bring honor to your name in all that I say and do.

Amen!

DAY 13

"MORE THAN AN EXPRESSION"

Proverbs 13:20
He who walks with the wise grows wise, but a companion of fools suffers harm.

"MORE THAN AN EXPRESSION"

"Show me your friends and I will show you your future," "birds of a feather flock together," "guilty by association." The list of sayings could go on and on, but the reality is that these mottos and this proverb is more than just a phrase; it is a truth to live by. I often look back at my younger years when I hung around with a less-than-godly group of people. This proverb was my reality; I suffered greatly because of my choice of friends.

One specific instance happened when I was 18. I entered a Rite Aid Pharmacy on Harford Road in Baltimore, MD with a "friend." Without my knowledge this young person had planned on shoplifting and shoplifting is what she did. On our way out of the store, we were stopped by Security, and both of us were arrested for shoplifting. It didn't matter that I was not the one stealing a curling iron (really, me? a guy, steal a curling iron of all things?). We were both charged. Who you choose to associate with will make you better or will bring you down. Choose to walk with the wise!

PRAYER

Father in heaven, I pray for discernment and wisdom in choosing my companions. Help me to surround myself with those who walk in righteousness, speak words of life, and inspire me to grow closer to You. Grant me the grace to be a positive influence on others, pointing them toward Your truth and love. Amen!

DAY 14

"THE SILENT JOY KILLER"

Proverbs 14: 30
A heart at peace gives life to the body, but envy rots the bones.

There is no greater joy-stealer than envy. It leads to bitterness, anger, and a feeling of inadequacy. Envy isn't just crushing to or emotions; it also causes our overall health and well-being to suffer by adding to the stresses and anxieties we already have.

In comparison, when we have contentment and peace in our hearts, we can have a vibrant life. We can enjoy the blessings that God has given us and appreciate the good things in our lives.

As Christians, we are called to be content in all things and it is our responsibility to find contentment and peace in our relationship with Jesus, regardless of our circumstances.

When we have a heart at peace, we are better able to hear God's voice and follow His will for our lives; we are able to trust in His plan for us and find joy in His presence.

PRAYER

Father in heaven, help me to guard my heart against envy and jealousy, give me the peace and contentment that comes from a heart that is satisfied with what I have, and teach me to rejoice in the blessings of others without feeling envious or resentful. Fill my heart with love, kindness, and generosity towards all those around me. Amen!

DAY 15

"BETTER THAN A FORTUNE COOKIE"

Proverbs 15: 22
Plans fail for lack of counsel, but with many advisers they succeed.

"BETTER THAN A FORTUNE COOKIE"

Can you imagine what your life would be like if you were able to actually know your future by what your fortune cookie said? I mean, how many times would we have made different decisions in life?

Clearly, we cannot see into the future or know all the possible outcomes of the decisions that we make based on a fortune cookie. We are wildly limited in our knowledge and understanding, which is why we must seek the advice and counsel of others who may have more experience or knowledge.

When we seek wise counsel, we gain new perspectives and insights that we may not have considered on our own. We are able to weigh the pros and cons of different options and make more informed decisions which in turn can save us from a lot of trouble and headaches.

If we want our plans to be successful, we must seek wisdom and understanding from God and from others, which is better than a fortune cookie.

PRAYER

Father in heaven, I seek your guidance and wisdom as I make decisions in my life. Help me to seek counsel from those who walk in righteousness so I make choices that align with your will and bring glory to your name. Amen!

DAY 16

"GOD BLESS THE REAL YOU"

Proverbs 16: 2 NIV
All a person's ways seem pure to them, but motives are weighed by the Lord.

"God blesses the real you, not the you you think you are." When my pastor dropped that little nugget of truth, I about fell out of my seat.

I have a tendency to justify my actions and believe that I am doing better than I am and doing things with the right intentions. We have all probably even deceived ourselves into thinking that our motives are pure and selfless. Whether that is true or not, God sees beyond what we do and say and into what is actually our hearts; He knows our true motives and intentions, even when we don't.

Nothing is hidden from God; He sees everything and knows everything. He cannot be deceived or manipulate by words or actions. The real us must be honest with ourselves and with God, examining our hearts and motives and seeking His guidance and direction.

PRAYER

Father in heaven, I surrender my plans and desires to you, recognizing that it is you who examines my motives and weighs my heart. Guide me in aligning my intentions with your perfect will so that my actions may bring honor and glory to you. Amen!

DAY 17

"WATERED DOWN WORDS"

Proverbs 17: 28
Even a fool is thought wise if he keeps his silent, and discerning if he holds his tongue.

"WATERED DOWN WORDS"

A great friend and mentor of mine once told me, "Do not water down your words." I had asked him how I was supposed to respond to a challenging situation that had come about in my ministry in which I felt pressured to give a response.

This wisdom has stuck with me and helped me throughout the years. What he was saying to me was to be careful to always give my opinion or share my thoughts about something because, in doing so, I have the potential to minimize the impact of my words.

So let's be more selective about what we use our words for!

PRAYER

Father in heaven, I humbly ask for the gift of wisdom and discernment in my speech and that I may think before I speak and choose words that bring healing, understanding, and peace. May my words be a reflection of your grace and love, and may they build up others and honor you. Amen!

DAY 18

"STICKS AND STONES"

Proverbs 18: 10
The name of the Lord is a strong tower; the righteous run to it and are safe.

Do you remember the phrase we used to say as kids, "Sticks and stone may break my bones but words will never hurt me." As we all know, that's simply not true; words are used daily to tear people down.

It is clear that words have the power to hurt people, but there is one word in this verse that has the power to protect people. It isn't so much a word as it is a name; the Lord. And it isn't just a name; it is a Person, the living Word, Jesus.

We face an insane amount of challenges and struggles; more often than not, we can feel overwhelmed by our circumstances and situations, and in these moments, it can be easy to feel alone and helpless.

But let me remind you of this; we are never alone! We can always find safety and protection in the name of the Lord. The name of the Lord is a strong tower, a place of refuge and safety when we seek Him. When we run to Him, we can find comfort, strength, and peace in the most difficult times of our lives. May we run to the strong tower of the Lord and find safety and protection in His name.

PRAYER

Father in heaven, I seek refuge in Your name, knowing that it is a strong tower where I find strength, protection, and unwavering support. Help me to continually find peace and security in Your presence. Amen!

DAY 19

"RAINBOWS AND UNICORNS"

Proverbs 19: 23
The fear of the Lord leads to life;
then one rests content,
untouched by trouble.

"RAINBOWS AND UNICORNS"

One of the greatest traps is to fall into the temptation to only pursue wealth, success, or pleasure, thinking that these things will bring us happiness and fulfillment, but anyone who has lived a little will tell us that these pursuits leave us feeling empty and unfulfilled.

True life and contentment come from having a healthy fear and respect for God. We are able to find true joy and fulfillment in Him rather than in the fleeting pleasures of this world. The blessings from God come when we honor Him with our lives.

Yes, it's true. Just because you honor God doesn't mean it's all rainbows and unicorns. Troubles will still come, but with God's help, we can face those challenges head-on.

So, let's embrace the joy of walking in the fear of the LORD.

PRAYER

Father in heaven, help me to be filled with reverence and awe towards You, understanding that the fear of the Lord is the beginning of wisdom and the foundation of a fruitful life. Guide me to live in a way that honors and pleases You.
Amen!

DAY 20

"UNDERPROMISE AND OVERDELIVER"

Proverbs 20: 25
It is a trap to dedicate something rashly and only later to consider one's vows.

One of my biggest character flaws is that I can be somewhat impulsive; when I say "somewhat," what I really mean is extremely. At times, we all tend to make impulsive decisions and commitments without fully considering the consequences. More often than not, it comes from good intentions. With a desire to be helpful, it is easy to make promises that we cannot keep. Many times we commit without fully understanding what is required.

I try to always under promise and over deliver. What that means is I try to always complete, help, serve or give more than I said I would. This keeps me from looking like a person who doesn't honor his word.

Let's make sure that we know all the detail and have sought God's guidance and wisdom in all that we do. We are called to be people of integrity and honesty, honoring our commitments and becoming more and more like Jesus!

PRAYER

Father in heaven, I pray for the wisdom to weigh my decisions carefully and the discernment to avoid the traps of hasty actions. Help me to trust in your guidance and to seek your will in all things, that I may honor you and bring glory to your name. Amen!

DAY 21

"WEAPON OF WISDOM"

Proverbs 21: 22
One who is wise can go up against the city of the mighty and pull down the stronghold in which they trust.

"WEAPON OF WISDOM"

When you think about waging war you are probably like me and think about some of the amazing weapons throughout history. I think of a samurai sword, a fighter jet or even David's slingshot.

This verse actually speaks of a different type of weapon, the weapon of wisdom. Wisdom is a weapon that has the power to overcome seemingly insurmountable obstacles.

Life comes with a crazy amount of challenges and obstacles and it is easy to feel overwhelmed by our circumstances. In these moments, it can be easy to feel discouraged and powerless.

This verse reminds us that wisdom is a powerful weapon that can help us overcome. When we are wise, we are able to see things from a different perspective and find creative solutions to the problems we face.

Rest assured, when we seek wisdom from God, He will give it to us generously.

PRAYER

Father in heaven, I humbly pray for strength and courage to face the challenges and strongholds in my life. Grant me the wisdom to wield the weapons of perseverance, faith, your truth, and wisdom so that I can overcome obstacles and experience victory in all areas of my life.

Amen!

DAY 22

"FRIENDS OF KINGS"

Proverbs 22: 11

One who loves a pure heart and who speaks with grace will have the king for a friend.

When I was growing up, I used to love going to this one friend's house because he had everything. His house was huge, he had a soccer goal, he had video games; it seemed as though he was living like a little kid king.

Clearly, this verse doesn't mean that because of your friend you're going to be sitting on a gold throne and commanding armies with your best friend or even living a lavish lifestyle. What it does mean is that if we not use our words wisely and also keep our hearts pure, we will have amazing relationships.

When we love others with a pure heart and when we speak with grace, we become people who people want to be around.

Let's be people who love others with a pure heart and speak with grace. When we do that, watch as the world becomes a better place—one joyful interaction at a time.

PRAYER

Father in heaven, I pray that you would cultivate within me a heart of purity and grace, that my words and actions may bring delight and favor to those around me. May my interactions be a reflection of your love, kindness, and righteousness, shining a light in this world.
Amen!

DAY 23

"WISDOM FROM THE BEATLES"

Proverbs 23: 4-5
Do not wear yourself out to get rich; do not trust your own cleverness. Cast but a glance at riches, and they are gone, for they will surely sprout wings and fly off to the sky like an eagle.

"WISDOM FROM THE BEATLES"

Before someone sends me an email, let me say this, this proverb isn't saying that wealth itself is a bad thing. It warns us about the danger of putting all our focus and energy into acquiring wealth and possessions, thinking that they will bring us happiness and fulfillment.

We have all heard the expression, "Money can't buy happiness." Or how about the wisdom from the Beatles, "Can't buy me love?" The things in life that are worth anything are the things money can't buy: love, joy, peace, meaningful relationships, and a relationship with Jesus.

Today is a good day to take a step back and look at our priorities. Let's not wear ourselves out trying to make more money and get more stuff but let's be intentional about cultivating a heart that treasures the things that truly matter.

PRAYER

Father in heaven, I surrender my desires for worldly wealth and success to you, recognizing that true treasure comes from seeking you above all else. Give me contentment and wisdom to steward my resources and time according to your purposes, trusting that you will provide abundantly and guide me in the path of true fulfillment. Amen!

49

"GUYS AND DIRECTIONS"

Proverbs 24: 6
Surely you need guidance to wage war, and victory is won through many advisers."

A tale as old as time... a man is lost but refuses to stop and ask for directions. Now, if you're from Generation Z or Generation Alpha, you have no idea what I am talking about. For the rest of us old people who lived before Waze, Maps and Google Maps, you know exactly what I am talking about. Man's inability to ask for help. As humans, not just males, we often think that we can handle things on our own and that seeking help or advice is a sign of weakness. I have found the truth to be the opposite of that; in order to be successful, especially in times of conflict or difficulty, we need to ask for direction.

The only way that we can gain new perspectives is when we actually seek guidance from others. You and I have very limited visibility; that is why it is so important that we have more perspectives than just ours. The wisdom and life experiences of others can greatly influence our lives for the better.

PRAYER

Father in heaven, I humbly seek your wisdom and understanding as I navigate the challenges and decisions that lie before me. Grant me discernment to build my life on a foundation of knowledge and guide my steps towards success, righteousness, and lasting fulfillment.
Amen!

DAY 25

"PEOPLE PROBLEMS"

Proverbs 25: 19
*Like a broken tooth or a lame
foot is reliance on the unfaithful
in a time of trouble.*

"PEOPLE PROBLEMS"

One of the greatest natural tendencies that God has placed in us is our natural need for community and companionship. One downfall with this is that when times of trouble come, it can be easy to look to people to alleviate some of our struggles and pain before we ever go to God.

We look to friends and family members, thinking that they will be there for us no matter what, and while most of the time that is true, there will be times when people fail us. Relying on those who are unfaithful or unreliable can cause more harm than good.

When we rely on these types of people we can be let down when they are not able to provide the support or guidance that we need. As Christians, we are called to trust in God and seek His guidance and direction, especially in times of trouble. When we trust in God and submit to His will, He will guide us and lead us to success.

PRAYER

Father in heaven, I bring before you any conflicts or discord in my relationships, asking for your peace to prevail. Grant me the wisdom to respond with kindness and patience, and help me to cultivate unity and harmony in all my interactions. Amen!

DAY 26

"MIND YA' BUSINESS"

Proverbs 26: 17
Like one who grabs a stray dog by the ears is someone who rushes into a quarrel not their own.

One of my favorite things to say to my daughter is, "Mind ya' business," in the most Italian-American accent I can muster up. She always has to be involved in whatever conversation her mother and I are having. This verse speaks to the danger of not minding ya' business.

I admit it is tempting to get involved in in other people's problems that don't have anything to do with us. Sometimes it's not from a place of wanting to be "in the know," sometimes, we feel obligated to defend others or to stand up for what's right, even if it means getting involved in a situation we're not in.

The verse warns against getting involved in arguments and conflicts that don't concern us. When we do, it's like grabbing a stray dog by the ear; you're going to get bit.

Let's never stop working towards peace and unity with others while using wisdom and discernment to know when and how to get involved.

PRAYER

Father in heaven, give me discernment and wisdom to know when to step forward and get involved in situations and when to exercise patience and trust in Your guidance. Help me make a positive impact according to Your will. Amen!

DAY 27
"LOPES' LESSON"

Proverbs 27: 12
The prudent see danger and take refuge, but the simple keep going and pay the penalty.

"LOPES' LESSON"

A great friend of mine, Eddies Lopes, who has now gone on to be with Jesus, would quote this verse all the time; this verse very clearly warns us about how important it is to be wise in our decision-making because when we are, it will help us recognize and avoid danger.

So often we are tempted to take risks or ignore warning signs, thinking that we can handle whatever comes our way. However, this verse reminds us that being prudent and recognizing danger can help us avoid paying the penalty or suffering harm.

When we are prudent and wise in our decision-making, we are able to recognize warning signs and take appropriate action to protect ourselves and others. We are able to make better decisions that honor God and reflect His will for our lives. Let's take Lopes' lesson to heart!

PRAYER

Father in heaven, I humbly seek your wisdom and discernment in all my decisions, knowing that my understanding is limited. Guide me away from paths that may lead to harm or regret, and direct me towards the choices that align with your perfect will, bringing blessings and fulfillment. Amen!

DAY 28

"HIDING FROM HEALING"

Proverbs 28: 13
Whoever conceals their sins does not prosper, but the one who confesses and renounces them finds mercy.

Recently I fell and scraped my side pretty badly. I tried to hide it from my wife because I knew if she found out, she was going to make me clean it out by pouring peroxide in it. The bad part about that was that the longer I kept hiding the scrape from her, the longer it took for it to heal.

This verse is very clear about the importance of confessing our sins and seeking forgiveness rather than trying to hide or conceal them. Like my scrape, we may be tempted to hide our sins or pretend that everything is okay, even when we know that we have done wrong. We may be afraid of the consequences or "spiritual peroxide" of our actions, or we may be ashamed of what we have done.

When we confess our sins and seek forgiveness, we are able to experience the grace and mercy of God and be reconciled to Him and to others. When we are honest and transparent about our mistakes and shortcomings, we are able to face the world with confidence and boldness rather than living in fear and shame.

Remember, God is faithful to forgive us and to cleanse us from all unrighteousness.

PRAYER

Father in heaven, I come before you with a repentant heart, acknowledging my shortcomings and sins. I humbly ask for your mercy, forgiveness, and the strength to walk in integrity, forsaking deceit and embracing a life of honesty and righteousness. Amen!

DAY 29

"ME MYSELF AND I"

Proverbs 29: 1
Whoever remains stiff-necked after many rebukes will suddenly be destroyed—without remedy.

"ME MYSELF AND I"

Have you ever heard the expression, "Me, myself and I?" I have heard people use that expression almost as a badge of courage, and that has always made me wonder why they are so proud to be alone.

I know, at times, we all like to make our own decisions, follow our own path and do things our own way, but this verse reminds us that we can't do it alone. There is no "me, myself, and I" in the Kingdom.

We make plans without seeking counsel from others, running the risk of missing important details, making mistakes, or in the wrong timing(this is a big one). When we seek advice from others, we can gain new perspectives, avoid pitfalls, and make better decisions.

Humility goes a long way; let's be people who are humble enough to seek advice from others. Let's surround ourselves with wise and trustworthy people who can offer us guidance and support. And when we make plans, let's make sure we're not doing it alone.

PRAYER

Father in heaven, I come before you with a humble heart, seeking your guidance and grace to avoid the pitfalls of stubbornness and pride. Help me to walk in humility and obedience, that I may find life, peace, and everlasting joy in your presence. Amen!

DAY 30

"SMART PHONES DUMB PEOPLE"

Proverbs 30: 5
Every word of God is flawless; he is a shield to those who take refuge in him.

In the day and age where everyone has a smartphone, you would think everyone would be "smart." Well, we all know that's not true. I mean we have ebooks, podcasts, google and forums on any topic you could imagine where we can seek out facts, history, wisdom and advice from others; so why then isn't everyone a genius? This verse answers that question. It doesn't matter how smart your phone is; the ultimate source of wisdom is God's word.

The Bible is not just any book - it's the living word of God; jam-packed with all the wisdom, guidance, and truth that we need to navigate life.

So let's stop going to inferior sources and make a commitment to read and study God's word. Let's seek wisdom from the ultimate source of wisdom; let's trust that every word of God is flawless and can guide us through life's ups and downs.

PRAYER

Father in heaven, I thank you for the gift of your word, which is pure, trustworthy and full of wisdom. I pray for a receptive heart and a teachable spirit that I may cling to your truth and find guidance and comfort in every season of life. Amen!

DAY 31

"WHAT WOULD YOU DO?"

Proverbs 31: 8
Speak up for those who cannot speak for themselves, for the rights of all who are destitute.

"WHAT WOULD YOU DO?"

Do you remember the show, What Would You Do? It was a popular and somewhat entertaining tv show that would stage issues happening in public and then film the people to see how they responded. Some people would intervene and speak and others would just walk on by.

This verse reminds me of that show and it reminds us that we have a responsibility to speak up for those who can't speak for themselves.

There are countless people groups in our world and communities who are marginalized, oppressed, and forgotten. Often times their rights are ignored or even violated. As followers of Jesus, we have a mandate from God to stand up for them and fight for justice.

So next time we see a situation where we need to speak up or intervene, let's be bold enough to do so. Let's use the voices God has given us to advocate for the marginalized, oppressed, and forgotten, and let's not just do it because it looks good on our social media but because it's what God calls us to do.

PRAYER

Father in heaven, I pray for a compassionate heart that champions the cause of the oppressed and speaks up for those who cannot speak for themselves. Grant me the courage and strength to be a voice for justice and a vessel of your love, shining your light in the darkest corners of the world.
Amen!

ABOUT THE
AUTHOR

Mike Badolato is the co-founder of Badolato Ministries, an evangelistic ministry that is focused on reaching the lost, bringing freedom to people who are bound, missions and awakening the Church. Mike passionately communicates the life and power of the Gospel across a diverse variety of life experiences. Mike's ministry is driven by a hunger for revival and a fresh move of God across the nation and this world.

Mike is happily married to his wife, Shari, and they have two children, Aiella and Alessio.

BADOLATO
MINISTRIES

www.badolatoministries.org

Made in United States
Troutdale, OR
11/24/2024

25272972R00042